# WEST BROMWICH
# ALBION
## THE OFFICIAL ANNUAL 2010

**g**

A Grange Publication

Written by Dave Bowler
Designed by Colin Heggie

© 2009. Published by Grange Communications Ltd., Edinburgh,
under licence from West Bromwich Albion Football Club plc.
Printed in the EU.

Photography by Laurie Rampling & Dave Bowler
Photographs © West Bromwich Albion Football Club Limited

ISBN 978-1-906211-91-2

£6.99

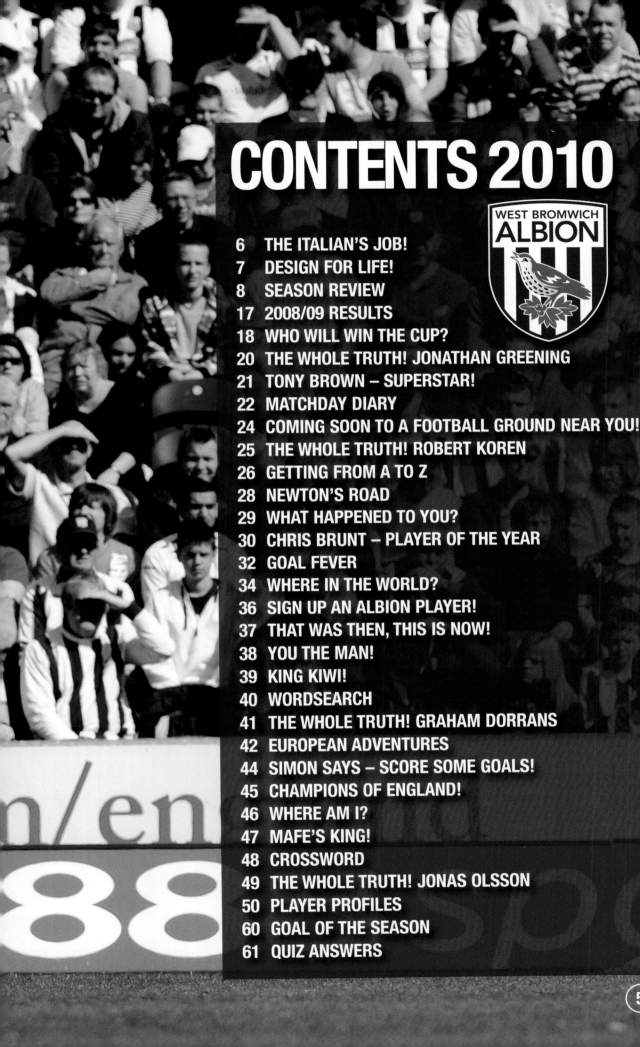

# CONTENTS 2010

**WEST BROMWICH ALBION**

# THE ITALIAN'S JOB!

**When the Albion were looking for a new head coach last summer, they could have hardly gone for a more high profile figure than Roberto Di Matteo.**

The former MK Dons gaffer enjoyed a high profile playing career with Lazio and Chelsea in particular, as well as playing for his country on 34 occasions, playing at both the European Championships of 1996 and the 1998 World Cup in France.

English fans know him best for his days with Chelsea though as a technically gifted attacking midfielder, Di Matteo winning the FA Cup twice with the London side, scoring in both finals at the old Wembley, the winner against Aston Villa in 2000 being the last cup final goal at the old stadium.

He also scored the fastest FA Cup Final goal beneath the Twin Towers in 1998, netting after 42 seconds against Middlesbrough, though Louis Saha surpassed that mark in last season's final for Everton.

Di Matteo's MK Dons reached the play-off finals last season, only to lose 7-6 on penalties to Scunthorpe United, but in qualifying, they scored 83 goals, the second best goalscoring record in England.

Good luck to Roberto in his new job at The Hawthorns – hopefully this year, he can go one better than last and clinch promotion!

# DESIGN FOR LIFE!

**What's Jono so upset about? Somebody's stolen his kit!**
It's up to you to design a new Albion away kit for him, any colour you like.

# SEASON REVIEW

**It all started in a spirit of hope in the blazing sunshine in the fanciest new stadium in the Premier League and it ended in the sunshine of homely Ewood Park, Throstles wearing Mowbray masks, beaten in the end, relegated to the Championship, but proud of our team and our football.**

## AUGUST

The Baggies were busy in the transfer market, bringing in England goalkeeper Scott Carson, Slovakian defender Marek Cech, Dutch under-21 full-back Gianni Zuiverloon and Ivory Coast centre-half Abdoulaye Meite before the big kick-off, with Jonas Olsson, Ryan Donk and Borja Valero – the club's record signing at £4.7million – all joining before the month was out.

Albion had the toughest start to the season possible, kicking off at the Emirates against Arsenal in the lunchtime game live on the telly. After ten minutes, any Albion fan might have been watching it from behind the sofa as Arsenal ripped the team to pieces and went 1-0 ahead. But after that, the Throstles gradually started to get into the game and might even have pinched a draw from Arsène Wenger's team before we finally had to submit to a 1-0 defeat.

A packed Hawthorns saw Albion play Everton off the park but come away beaten thanks to some bad defensive mistakes, something that would become a theme for the season. Roman Bednar got Albion's first goal of the campaign, but a 2-1 defeat was a big disappointment for everyone after Albion had played so well.

Defeat in extra time at Hartlepool United in the League Cup wasn't that great a loss, and we did at least see a wonderful goal from Robert Koren, but Albion went to Bolton on the following Saturday desperate to get a first point of the season. We went into the two week international break having done just that, drawing 0-0 at the Reebok, though again we were easily the better team. Kim Do-Heon hit the bar with a screamer, then Ishmael Miller couldn't finish off a great chance as the game ended up without a goal.

## SEPTEMBER

The first win of the season came in an action-packed game with West Ham, neither side having a sponsor on their shirts after the Hammers' sponsor went bust – they played the game with a claret patch over the logo! It was a real cracker of a game see-sawing back and forwards before Chris Brunt finally sealed the three points for the Baggies late on.

A defeat at home to Villa is never a good thing to think about, so moving quickly on, we went up north to Middlesbrough and got our first – and only – away win in the Premiership. Jonas Olsson scored his first goal for the club to win it and after that, the game went crazy. Middlesbrough were camped in Albion's penalty area and could easily have had two or three goals, but on the breakaway, Albion could have had six. How the game ended 1-0 is still a mystery.

## OCTOBER

The month started well with a very controlled performance against Fulham, especially after half-time. The Throstles won that 1-0, thanks to a goal from Roman Bednar again, and we went off into another international break in great spirits and in 9th place in the league.

Unfortunately we lost our momentum in the break, though it didn't help that Manchester United were waiting for us when we started up again. We were well in the game for an hour at Old Trafford, but Wayne Rooney was in irresistible form and in the end, United were too strong for us. The week after, we went on the rampage against Hull, completely battered them for the first 45 minutes, but somehow, we lost 3-0 at home to them. That turned out to be a very important result at the end of the season.

We had a nightmare start to the midweek game at Newcastle, losing 2-0 at half-time and playing badly, but we were much better after the break and deserved more than just Ishmael Miller's consolation goal in the second half. We didn't get what we deserved a lot of the time this season, but such is life. All you can do is keep trying your best!

## NOVEMBER

We were robbed! Against Blackburn at The Hawthorns, our visitors were given the softest penalty in the first few minutes and then, after the Baggies had fought back to take the lead, a long range shot deep into injury time flew past Scott Carson and into the bottom corner to end things at 2-2. There's no justice! Robbie Keane – he was at Liverpool then – did

his usual act against the Albion and scored two goals as we were beaten 3-0 at Anfield and after that, we had Chelsea at The Hawthorns. Who was sorting out this fixture list?! We competed well against Chelsea – just as we had against Liverpool - but the game finished with the same result, Albion on the wrong end of a 3-0 defeat.

Going to Stoke... we might as well not bother, we never win there! There was nothing between the teams going into the last ten minutes when the Throstles had a penalty appeal turned down. A couple of minutes later, Stoke went up the other end and scored and we'd lost in the Potteries once again.
But if you thought that was bad, you hadn't seen anything yet. Wigan was worse – not that you could see much of that because of the thick fog that covered the JJB Stadium. If it had been a boxing match, it would have been stopped ages before the end to save Wigan taking more punishment. But all we had to show for it was a single goal from Miller and a couple of late mistakes at the back saw the Baggies coming home beaten 2-1 and stuck on the bottom of the table. It was good to see the back of November.

## DECEMBER

Things were a little bit better against Portsmouth at the start of December, the Throstles ending the run of four straight defeats by getting a draw at The Hawthorns, Jonathan Greening getting a rare goal for Albion. Once again we should probably have got a better result, but you couldn't say that about the game at Sunderland a week later. We were terrible! It was just one of those days where nothing went right for Albion and everything Sunderland hit went in the net. A 4-0 defeat was a pretty fair scoreline. And it was a long way home.

The richest football club in the world came to West Bromwich to help us celebrate Christmas, and celebrate we did! We beat Manchester City much more easily than the 2-1 score suggests we did, outplaying an expensively assembled side to give us real hope of another "Great Escape" for the Baggies in 2009. We'd done it before – we could do it again!

Boxing Day at Chelsea didn't help things very much it's true, but after we had lost narrowly in the capital, we were quickly back on track at The Hawthorns, beating up Chelsea's local

neighbours Tottenham. We had to wait until the last seven minutes for the goals to come, but come they did thanks to Roman Bednar and Craig Beattie and as we left the Albion ground, with three more points in our pockets, 2008 seemed like it had been a pretty good year all round. We were even off the bottom!

## JANUARY

The FA Cup kicked in on the first Saturday of the New Year and, just as we seemed to be on our way to round four, leading 1-0 at home to Peterborough, we let in a late goal to go to a replay. Loan signing Jay Simpson and Paul Robinson saw us through that one but it was an extra game we didn't need, especially as in between times, we had been beaten at Villa Park in another very close derby game.

If we had only realised at the time that the 3-0 win over Middlesbrough was probably the season's highest point, maybe we would have enjoyed it even more. It was the first time we'd ever won three consecutive home games in the Premier League, the first time we'd ever done the double over Premiership opponents and, to top it all, it was a brilliant performance. We simply smashed Middlesbrough, new loan signing Marc-Antoine Fortune scoring, as did Robert Koren and Chris Brunt, though Brunt's goal was later changed to a Boro own goal by the goal panel.

We were off the bottom and going well, but the FA Cup disrupted things, Albion only drawing at home to Burnley. Worse yet, Jonas Olsson, our most consistent performer at the back, got injured and had to sit out ten games. In the end, it might have been that injury that sent Albion down because with Jonas in the team, don't you think we would have got four or five more points in those games?

January ended on a real low with the visit of Manchester United. A string of terrible decisions, including the crazy red card for Paul Robinson that was later overturned, meant that Albion never had a chance against the champions, and we were well beaten, 5-0. We did get some comfort though with the trip to Hull, thousands of Baggies descending on the KC Stadium courtesy of free travel. Albion struggled early on but responded to the great support by grabbing a 2-2 draw with goals from Simpson and Brunt, keeping themselves in the survival race.

## FEBRUARY

An icy night in Burnley saw the end of our FA Cup hopes, but we were all focusing on the crunch game with Newcastle at The Hawthorns on the Saturday. A win against a team that was dropping like a stone would

have spread a huge wave of optimism about the club, but some comical defending – though we weren't laughing at the time – meant that we were beaten by the Toon, and that was before Alan Shearer had turned up.

A break for the FA Cup saw us leave the country for a spot of extra training but it did us no good. We were beaten 2-0 at Fulham and if their goalposts hadn't been in such good form, it might have been a lot worse! We were in better form at Everton, even their manager David Moyes admitted we were the better side, but that was a 2-0 defeat too and we were in trouble.

## MARCH

The Throstles were in good form against Arsenal, but the Gunners were that bit better and although Chris Brunt equalised their early opener, two goals just before half-time saw us off. By the time we went down to West Ham, we'd reached the point of no return – after four league defeats, we couldn't lose again.

With surprise call ups for Shelton Martis and Graham Dorrans, the Baggies were completely on top right through the game but... you guessed, we didn't get what we deserved, coming away with only a 0-0 draw. It was the same story against Bolton at home, completely outplaying them, but only a 1-1 draw to show for it.

## APRIL

We started April with a must-win game against Stoke. But you know what always happens against Stoke, and it happened again. So we went to Portsmouth and really did need a win. We outclassed them on their own pitch and even Jonathan Greening scored, but we still couldn't get the win and had to make do with a 2-2 draw. It was even more frustrating a week later when some bad luck and bad refereeing decisions saw us beaten at Manchester City having again deserved lot more from the day – for about the 20th time that season!

There was no question about it when Sunderland came to the Black Country. We had to beat them. And we did! It was 3-0 going on 10, revenge for the game on Wearside before Christmas. Albion weren't finished yet!

## MAY

There haven't been many times when Albion have played better in the Premier League than at Tottenham but, yet again, luck was not on our side and we lost 1-0, even Harry Redknapp finding it impossible to believe that his side had won.

But back we boinged again, strolling to a 3-0 win over Wigan and still we had hope of surviving. Sadly, that ended the following Sunday when we gifted Liverpool the first goal of the game and ended up being beaten. Even then, the support that the players got at the end of the game was simply magnificent, a reflection of all the entertainment they'd given us all season.

Yes, winning is important, but sometimes it's the way you play the game that matters most of all!

# 2008/09 RESULTS

| DATE | OPPONENTS | RESULT | SCORERS |
|------|-----------|--------|---------|
| Sat Aug 16th | Arsenal | 0-1 | |
| Sat Aug 23rd | EVERTON | 1-2 | Bednar |
| Tue Aug 26th | Hartlepool United (Carling Cup 2) | 1-3 | Koren |
| Sat Aug 30th | Bolton Wanderers | 0-0 | |
| Sat Sep 13th | WEST HAM UNITED | 3-2 | Morrison, Bednar, Brunt |
| Sun Sep 21st | ASTON VILLA | 1-2 | Morrison |
| Sat Sep 27th | Middlesbrough | 1-0 | Olsson |
| Sat Oct 4th | FULHAM | 1-0 | Bednar |
| Sat Oct 18th | Manchester United | 0-4 | |
| Sat Oct 25th | HULL CITY | 0-3 | |
| Tue Oct 28th | Newcastle United | 1-2 | Miller |
| Sat Nov 1st | BLACKBURN ROVERS | 2-2 | Bednar, Miller |
| Sat Nov 8th | Liverpool | 0-3 | |
| Sat Nov 15th | CHELSEA | 0-3 | |
| Sat Nov 22nd | Stoke City | 0-1 | |
| Sat Nov 29th | Wigan Athletic | 1-2 | Miller |
| Sun Dec 7th | PORTSMOUTH | 1-1 | Greening |
| Sat Dec 13th | Sunderland | 0-4 | |
| Sun Dec 21st | MANCHESTER CITY | 2-1 | Moore, Bednar |
| Fri Dec 26th | Chelsea | 0-2 | |
| Sun Dec 28th | TOTTENHAM HOTSPUR | 2-0 | Bednar, Beattie |
| Sat Jan 3rd | PETERBOROUGH UNITED (FA Cup 3) | 1-1 | Olsson |
| Sat Jan 10th | Aston Villa | 1-2 | Morrison |
| Tue Jan 13th | Peterborough United (FA Cup 3 replay) | 2-0 | Simpson, Robinson |
| Sat Jan 17th | MIDDLESBROUGH | 3-0 | Fortune, Koren, own goal |
| Sat Jan 24th | BURNLEY (FA Cup 4) | 2-2 | Koren, Kim |
| Tue Jan 27th | MANCHESTER UNITED | 0-5 | |
| Sat Jan 31st | Hull City | 2-2 | Simpson, Brunt |
| Tue Feb 3rd | Burnley (FA Cup 4 replay) | 1-3 | Zuiverloon |
| Sat Feb 7th | NEWCASTLE UNITED | 2-3 | Fortune 2 |
| Sun Feb 22nd | Fulham | 0-2 | |
| Sat Feb 28th | Everton | 0-2 | |
| Tue Mar 3rd | ARSENAL | 1-3 | Brunt |
| Mon Mar 16th | West Ham United | 0-0 | |
| Sat Mar 21st | BOLTON WANDERERS | 1-1 | Koren |
| Sat Apr 4th | STOKE CITY | 0-2 | |
| Sat Apr 11th | Portsmouth | 2-2 | Greening, Brunt |
| Sat Apr 18th | Manchester City | 2-4 | Brunt 2 |
| Sat Apr 25th | SUNDERLAND | 3-0 | Olsson, Brunt, Menseguez |
| Sat May 2nd | Tottenham Hotspur | 0-1 | |
| Sat May 9th | WIGAN ATHLETIC | 3-1 | Fortune 2, Brunt |
| Sun May 17th | LIVERPOOL | 0-2 | |
| Sun May 24th | Blackburn Rovers | 0-0 | |

# WHO WILL WIN

**The 2010 World Cup in South Africa is nearly here, but who's going to win it?**

Will Italy retain the title? Will the hosts become the first African nation ever to lift the trophy? What about the challenge from Brazil and Argentina?

Or will Fabio's boys be absolutely fabulous and win it for England?

We asked some of the Albion players who they think will be picking up the greatest prize in world sport in the summer…

**GIANNI ZUIVERLOON:**
I'm going to say Holland of course!

**NEIL CLEMENT:**
It's always the big guns, but England are playing well so I'm going to go with us.

**JONAS OLSSON:**
Sweden! Well, I hope they will. My heart says Sweden so I hope they have a chance.

# THE CUP?

**CHRIS WOOD:**
I would like it to be New Zealand if we qualify, otherwise I hope it will be England.

**DEAN KIELY:**
Ireland because that's my country. I think the squad of players we have got at the moment could do it.

**GRAHAM DORRANS:**
Brazil are always strong candidates, but I hope to see England do well.

**ISHMAEL MILLER:**
I would say Argentina. They have some great young players coming up. They won the Olympics last year and by the World Cup those players will be older, wiser and more experienced. They stand a good chance.

# JONATHAN GREENING

# THE WHOLE TRUTH!

**Who first kicked a ball around with you?**
My brothers, in the backyard and down at the park. We probably kicked it around in the hall and smashed all my mum's stuff! I've got one older and two younger brothers and a sister too!

**Did you play in your school football team and if so from what age and what position?**
I played in my primary school team when I was about seven. It was the full team, with players four years older than me. That was the first time I played in school football. I played all through secondary school too. I was a striker then.

**Do you have any tattoos? If so, what are they of?**
I've got a fair few! I've got my kids' names and birthdays. I've got some angels too, mainly on my arms, but I've got some on my back.

**What is your favourite stadium other than The Hawthorns?**
It has to be Old Trafford, especially when it's a full house - it's unbelievable. It's a great place to play. That's why they call it the 'Theatre of Dreams'.

**Who is your biggest influence in the game?**
Probably my mum and dad when I was little. They ran me around, always believed in me and supported me throughout my career. They have always been there for me to talk to about everything.

**Have you ever played as yourself on any football computer game?**
No, I'm not really a computer-game person. I had a little bash on Mario Kart during our pre-season tour but I came last in every game so I chucked my Nintendo DS in the bin! I didn't really! I gave it to one of my kids because I was so bad.

**When you eventually hang up your boots what would you like to do?**
I'd like to stay in the game, either by coaching or through the media, like doing radio commentary on games. You are a long time retired and I couldn't do nothing at all. I'd be bored out my mind! I love football that much it would be hard not to stay involved.

# TONY BROWN
# SUPER STAR!

**The Walk of Stars in Birmingham's Broad Street wanted to honour an Albion player on its walkway in 2009, so it asked the supporters to cast their votes as to who should receive the star.**

The overwhelming favourite was Tony Brown – and quite right too! As the Baggies' greatest goalscorer and the man who has played more games for the Throstles than anybody else, who else could it have been?

He received his star at half-time during the Liverpool game at the end of the 2008/09 season, and well chuffed he was too!

"I can't tell you how pleased and humbled I was. The fact that it was voted for by the supporters is what makes it so special because I've been lucky enough to have a great bond with the fans both as a player and ever since I finished as well.

"They've been great to me and it is a special thing, a great honour, to win any award that they vote for. It means a great deal. I just hope I have given them as much back as they've given to me.

"I may not have been the best player Albion have ever had, but I don't think there have been any more loyal. And that's what this game is about, loyalty. There's nothing more important than standing by your club."

# MATCHDAY DIARY

Having a rest

We're not letting you in!

Kitted out

Always thinking

Looking up

CAPTAIN

Two for the head one for the arm

**We all know what happens for 90 minutes of matchday, but what happens around the stadium before and during the game? We took a look…**

The best food!

Read all about it!

He looks familiar!

Say cheese!

Goal!

# COMING SOON
## TO A FOOTBALL GROUND NEAR YOU!

**Pre-season training is a great opportunity for the younger players at the Albion to mix with the more senior pros and to make a big impression on them – and the new head coach!**

Last July was no exception and youngsters like David Worrall, Romaine Sawyers, Lateef Elford-Alliyu, Josh Knight and Dwayne Samuels all took full advantage of some extended training sessions

under the gaze of Roberto Di Matteo and his coaching staff, Eddie Newton, Michael Appleton and Ade Mafe.

**So remember those names – they might be wearing the stripes pretty soon!**

# THE WHOLE TRUTH!

## ROBERT KOREN

**My proudest moment was...**
When my son was born. In football I would say it was winning the Championship title - that was a good day.

**I always laugh at...**
My son! It doesn't matter what's happened in my day he always puts a smile on my face. In the dressing room, it is Robbo and Dean Kiely. They have very good banter. Before it was obviously Zoltan Gera!

**My favourite restaurant is...**
Any Italian restaurant as I love Italian food, or TGI Friday's.

**To wake myself up I...**
Don't need to set my alarm because I have a two-year-old son, Nal, who wakes me up every morning at 7am.

**If I could be anyone else I would be...**
My wife, to see what it is like to live with me and see everything from the other side.

**The best thing my parents taught me is...**
To be a nice person and be proud of myself and what I'm doing. Also, to be nice to others and they will be nice to you too.

**It's not good for my image but I like...**
Watching cartoons with my boy. I like Disney the best, especially Mickey Mouse!

**1** A former World Cup winner who later managed the Albion.

**2** One of our nicknames.

**3** Our England goalkeeper.

**4** The capital of Dean Kiely's international country.

**5** The team we beat in the 1968 FA Cup Final.

**6** How many did we score against Coventry and Bristol Rovers in the 2008 FA Cup?

**7** Captain marvel!

**8** Home sweet home!

**9** Albion defender Larus Sigurdsson came from this country.

**10** Astle's first name.

**11** Nearby club where we play some of our reserve games.

**12** From which club did we buy Robert Koren?

**13** Mr. Ishmael?

**14** Our opponents on the first day of the 2009/10 season.

**15** Swedish central defender.

**16** We've beaten them in two FA Cup Finals!

**17** Who did we beat to clinch the Championship in 2008?

**18** Our manager for the "Great Escape".

**19** Opposite the Brummie.

**20** Another nickname!

**21** Nigerian full-back from our first Premiership season.

**22** Our most expensive signing.

**23** Albion's captain in the late 1970s and early 1980s.

**24** If an Albion player breaks a bone, he has one of these in hospital.

**25** Another name for the Under 18s team.

**26** Dutch full-back who played at the Beijing Olympics.

ANSWERS ON P

# A TO Z

We're going from A to Z with the Albion with this quiz — 26 questions, each featuring a different letter of the Albion alphabet. Do you know your Baggies letters?

# NEWTON'S ROAD

**Eddie Newton is another of the new faces at The Hawthorns after all the comings and goings last summer, joining the Throstles with Roberto Di Matteo as assistant head coach.**

Off the pitch, Newton teamed up with Di Matteo at MK Dons in the summer of 2008 and when the Italian moved to The Hawthorns, Newton swiftly agreed to move with him.

But the pair first met as players at Stamford Bridge in 1996 when big-name signing Di Matteo arrived from Lazio to team up with established home-grown midfielder Newton.

They struck up a formidable partnership and both men scored in the club's 2-0 1997 FA Cup Final success over Middlesbrough.

Born on December 13, 1971, in Hammersmith, Newton came through the ranks at Chelsea as a player. He was loaned out to Cardiff in January 1992, scoring four goals in 18 games, before returning to West London.

On the international front he was capped by England Under-21s twice.

In 1998 he helped Chelsea win the UEFA Cup Winners' Cup and the League Cup but the arrival of French World Cup-winning midfielder Didier Deschamps limited his first-team chances and in July 1999 he moved to Birmingham City, where he spent six months.

Short spells at Oxford United, Barnet and Hayes followed and he finished with a career record of 259 appearances, including 41 as a substitute, and 14 goals.

# WHAT HAPPENED TO YOU?

Some of our player pictures have been sabotaged. Either they've been cut up or they've been distorted on the computer.

Can you help us work out who's who?

ANSWERS ON P61

29

# CHRIS BRUNT
# PLAYER OF THE YEAR

**As ever, it was left to the Albion players and coaching staff to cast their votes to decide who was going to be selected as our Player of the Season after the rigours of the year in the Premier League.**

After the votes were counted, Chris Brunt was selected by a landslide majority, and little wonder after finishing at the top of the goalscoring pile from a midfield position – just like Tony Brown used to do!

Chris was in and out of the side a little bit at the start of the season as Albion experimented with playing four or five midfielders, Brunt often the one to miss out. But it soon became clear that with his ability to pick a pass or sling in a perfect cross with his wand of a left foot, Brunty was the man most likely to create chances for the Throstles.

A dead eye from free-kicks, Chris caused all kinds of goalkeepers all kinds of trouble from set pieces, but as the season went on, manager Tony Mowbray made a crucial switch, putting the left footed Chris on the right wing.

It seemed a weird move, but with Chris able to drift inside and hit shots at goal with his left peg, it brought goal after goal. Even though the dubious goal panel pinched his strike against Middlesbrough off him – and Graham Dorrans cheekily tried to steal the goal at Portsmouth! – Chris finished top of the goalscoring charts as well as Player of the Season.

Now all he has to do is do it again!

# GOAL FEVER

Getting goals in the Premier League is a tough job, but with our attacking style of play, we still found the back of the net plenty of times. What about these for a glut of goals!?

# WHERE IN THE WORLD?

**Which holiday destinations do our players fancy trying out – who knows, you might have already been there!**

nice, quiet break.
I think it would be a place to get away from everything and just relax.

SCOTT CARSON: Somewhere like Mauritius for a

Las Vegas.
I would love to go there.
It looks amazing and like my sort of scene.

ISHMAEL MILLER:

DEAN KIELY: Australia, to do some travelling around there.

I also have some relatives there so it would be nice to spend time with them.

Miami — I hear it's very nice and Disney World isn't far from there!

JONAS OLSSON: I would love to go to Africa on safari.

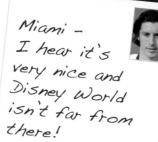

CHRIS BRUNT: The west coast of America to

visit Los Angeles and San Francisco. I'd like to go to the other coast, to New York too.

# SIGN UP AN ALBION PLAYER!

**I BET you thought you knew everything there was to know about every Albion player – but we've got a new one to tell you about – 'Albion Player'.**

Albion Player is the brand new name for Albion World - and a brand new name means a brand new look. Player will be bigger, literally, with a larger, clearer picture and boasts near-DAB quality audio commentary. And even Mac users can join in the fun now.

Albion Player brings you regular interviews from the training ground, before and after match features, extended highlights, Q&A sessions and live commentary of every Albion game, wherever and whenever it takes place.

So get yourself signed up to Albion Player at
**www.wba.co.uk**

# THAT WAS THEN
# THIS IS NOW

**The way we get to football matches has changed a lot over the last years, as these two pictures of Albion fans following their team shows!**

The first group are pictured on a train station platform, done out in their best Albion scarves and rosettes ahead of the trip to Wembley Stadium for the FA Cup final on 1st May, 1954.

A bit more up to date, pictured in front of the Baggies Travel coaches are a group of supporters who took advantage of the free coach travel up to the Premiership game at Hull City in January 2009.

**Which only goes to prove that we will follow the Albion, over land and sea – and water!**

# YOU THE MAN!

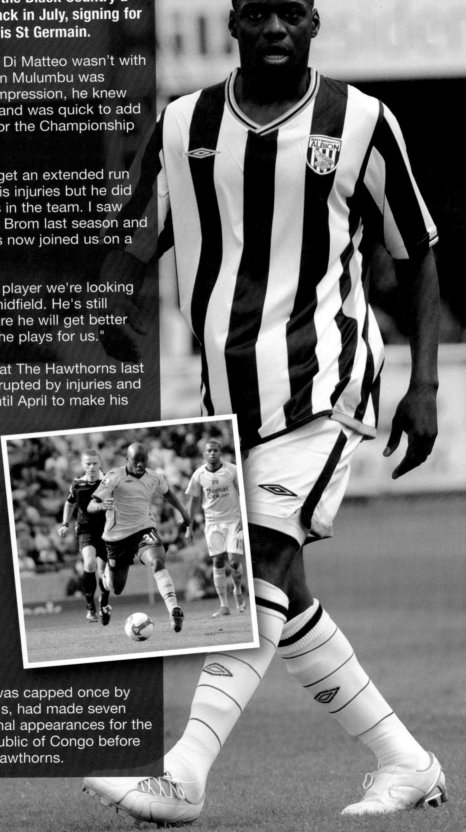

One of Albion's loan signing successes from last season, Youssouf Mulumbu, made his move to the Black Country a permanent deal back in July, signing for £175,000 from Paris St Germain.

Although Roberto Di Matteo wasn't with the Throstles when Mulumbu was making such an impression, he knew plenty about him and was quick to add him to his plans for the Championship season ahead.

"Youssouf didn't get an extended run last year due to his injuries but he did well when he was in the team. I saw him play for West Brom last season and I'm delighted he's now joined us on a permanent basis.

"He could be the player we're looking for in defensive midfield. He's still young and I'm sure he will get better the more games he plays for us."

Mulumbu's spell at The Hawthorns last season was interrupted by injuries and he had to wait until April to make his Barclays Premier League debut, coming on as a sub in a 2-2 draw at Portsmouth. In total, Mulumbu made six appearances, including four as a sub, and caught the eye with his energetic midfield performances.

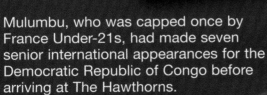

Mulumbu, who was capped once by France Under-21s, had made seven senior international appearances for the Democratic Republic of Congo before arriving at The Hawthorns.

# KING
## KIWI!

**2009 was a pretty decent year for Albion starlet Chris Wood.**

He completed his first season in the Albion Academy, scored a hatful of goals for the reserves and the youth team, and became the youngest ever debutant for the Baggies in the Premier League, as a second half sub at Portsmouth. He was only the fifth New Zealander ever to play in the Premiership.

Not content with that, he signed his first professional contract, and was named the Nike Young Men's Player of the Year at the 2008 New Zealand Football (NZF) Awards luncheon in Auckland.

And still it wasn't over for Chris. He got a call up to the full New Zealand national squad and spent June in South Africa as part of the Confederations Cup team.

So if he managed all that in 2009, who knows what 2010 will bring?!

# WORD**SEARCH**

**Why is the Albion dressing room deserted? Because all the players are out looking for these lost words! Give them a hand will you!?**

```
S H E P H E R D V G F
B H J Y D R X N W B A
A G S F H J M R E B C
S B C T E M B U S D U
T D A P G A T E S F P
L O R D L R D X K L S
E V S H J T U K F K W
B M O R R I S O N Y O
V A N Y U S Y R T R O
G K W A P G Y E L O D
H A W T H O R N S G I
```

**ASTLE**
**CARSON**
**FA CUP**
**GATES**

**HAWTHORNS**
**KOREN**
**LORD**
**MARTIS**

**MORRISON**
**SHEPHERD**
**WBA**
**WOOD**

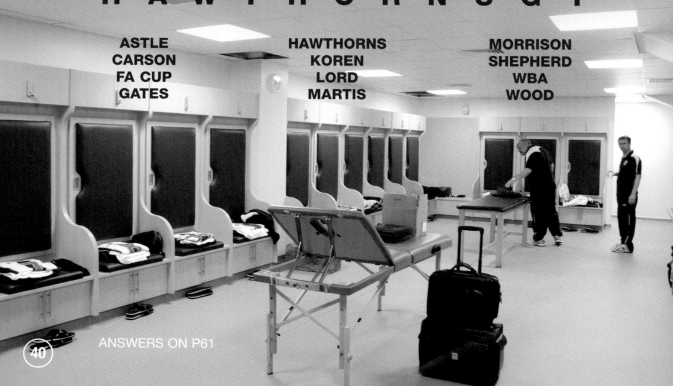

ANSWERS ON P61

# THE WHOLE TRUTH!

## GRAHAM DORRANS

**What's your earliest memory?**
I had a season ticket for Rangers with my dad, so my first memory is being taken to Ibrox for a match. I can't remember which one it was though!

**Did you ever collect football stickers/cards when you were a child, and if so did you ever complete an album?**
I collected them when I was at school and me and my mates did swaps. I did actually finish a few albums.

**Do you have any tattoos? If so, what are they of?**
No. I'm not sure if I would have one because I'm not a big fan of needles!

**What is your favourite stadium other than The Hawthorns?**
Being Scottish and a Rangers supporter I would have to say Ibrox! It holds special memories as I'm a fan. I also like Liverpool so I'm going to say Anfield as well. There is always a good atmosphere there.

**When you eventually hang up your boots what would you like to do?**
Hopefully I'll have a holiday home somewhere sunny and I can just go there and relax. I haven't even thought about after my career yet, but maybe I could get involved in coaching with a team in Spain somewhere!

# EUROPEAN ADVENTURES

**Getting into Europe is the big hope for every team when you start out on a new season and while the Throstles' only chance of qualifying for next season is by winning a cup, we've plenty of history in the competitions to look back on.**

It all started more than 40 years ago, in 1966/67, when the Baggies took part in the Inter-Cities Fairs Cup. That was the competition that eventually became the UEFA Cup, which has now been replaced by the Europa League. Confused yet?!

Our first official venture onto foreign fields took us to Holland, where we drew 1-1 with DOS Utrecht, Bobby Hope scoring our first Euro goal. We beat them 5-2 back at The Hawthorns, Tony Brown getting our first, and so far only, European hat-trick. We were able to put the passports away after the next round though - we were beaten 6-1 on aggregate by Italian side Bologna.

Two years later, we were in the Cup Winners' Cup, a competition that has long since disappeared. The first round saw us go to Belgium for "the battle of Bruges", an ill-tempered game that saw Jeff Astle knocked out and the opposition supporters pelting the players as they left the field. Albion won through on Asa Hartford's away goal, then beat Dinamo Bucharest of Romania with bags to spare, 5-1.

In the quarter-final, we were up against Dunfermline Athletic, and after drawing 0-0 in Scotland, looked set to go through. But on one of the coldest nights ever at the Albion, we froze and lost 1-0!

It was ten years before we were back in Europe, for perhaps our greatest season, 1978/79 in the UEFA Cup. We started off in Turkey, at Galatasaray, the club now infamous for those "Welcome to Hell" banners! It wasn't that bad for the Baggies and we won 3-1 and then did the same back in England. Off to Portugal next, winning 2-0 at SC Braga, then 1-0 at The Hawthorns.

That gave us one of the biggest games in our history, against Spanish giants Valencia, led by the man who had only just won the World Cup for Argentina, the brilliant goalscorer Mario Kempes. Everybody reckoned Valencia would win the competition that year, but Laurie Cunningham was magnificent as Albion got a 1-1 draw in Valencia, then two goals from Tony Brown saw them off at The Hawthorns.

Red Star Belgrade of the then Yugoslavia were our quarter-final opposition. Albion played in front of a crowd of over 95,000 in Belgrade and were beaten by a single goal. Cyrille Regis got us level at home and the game looked set for extra time until Red Star got a lucky goal in the last few minutes and went through.

A couple of European seasons have come and gone since then, both marked by first round defeats – Carl Zeiss Jena in 1979/80 and Grasshoppers of Zurich in 1981/82 – but who knows? One day, the Throstles might be playing in the Europa League!

# SIMON SAYS!
## SCORE SOME GOALS ■

Albion were busy in the transfer market last summer, drafting in goalscorer Simon Cox from Swindon Town for £1.9million, ending a long chase for one of League One's hottest properties – and that was where head coach Roberto Di Matteo spotted him, as Cox says.

"When I was at Swindon we played the gaffer's MK Dons side twice and they played good football, he did the same at Chelsea so that's his style. He doesn't want to launch the ball up in the air and make people run after it.

"It will be a step up because the players are obviously going to be technically better - but it won't be a massive step up. When you're playing in a big side in the Championship who have come down from the Premier League people are going to raise their game against us. We need to match that and with work ethic, and the quality we've got in the squad, we should win games."

Cox is a big admirer of former England, Manchester United and Tottenham striker Teddy Sheringham, and he hopes that his move to The Hawthorns is part of a learning curve en route to a similar career.

"I enjoyed watching Teddy Sheringham and the way he plays the game. His mind is second to none and he played on until he was 40. If I can have any sort of career like that I'll have done alright!"

# CHAMPIONS OF ENGLAND!

**This season is the 90th anniversary of when the Throstles won the old First Division for the first, and only, time.**

The 1919/20 season was extraordinary in many ways. It was the first season of proper football after World War One had ended, the first chance for people to get back to watching the national game all over again.

Because of the break for the war, teams had changed dramatically from those that had taken to the field back in 1914/15, so everything was up for grabs.

It was the Baggies who did the grabbing, winning nine of the first 11 games to leave everybody trailing behind them, scoring goals like it was going out of fashion. They beat Notts County 8-0, and, over the course of the season, put five past Everton, Blackburn Rovers (twice) and scored four on 11 other occasions.

By the end of the campaign, the Throstles had amassed a record 60 points, scored 104 goals, won 28 games and were the Champions of England by nine clear points, ahead of Burnley in second place. Captain Jesse Pennington lifted the championship trophy and the Baggies were the best team around.

Sadly, we didn't see the trophy again until Jonathan Greening got hold of it at QPR in May 2008, now the prize for winning the Football League Championship. Same again this year?

# WHERE AM I ?

**As you can see, Ishmael needs a bit of a rest – can you help him find his way back to the dressing room?**

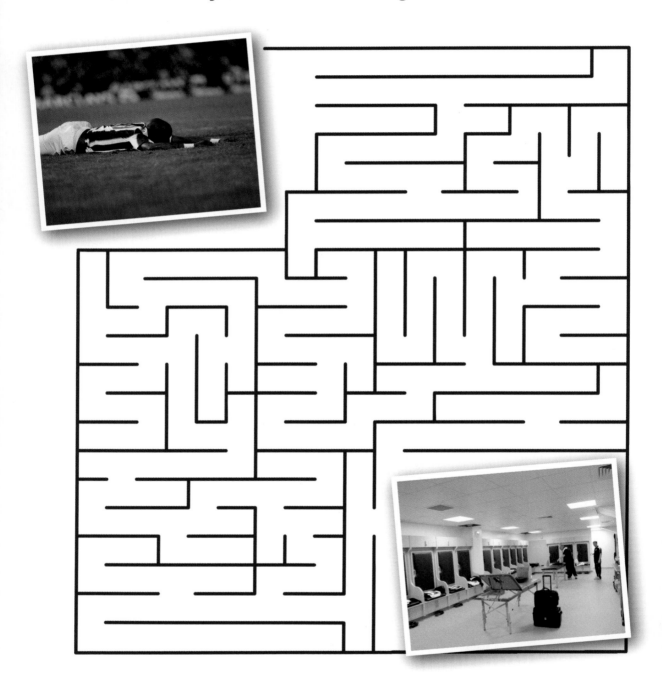

ANSWERS ON P61

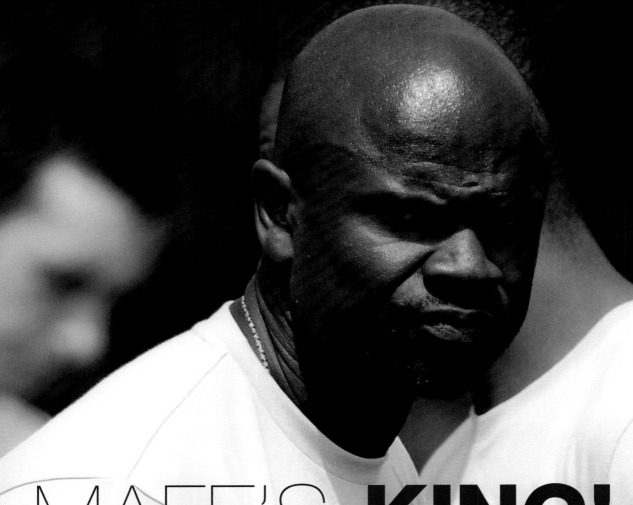

# MAFE'S KING!

**If you see any of the Albion players walking away from the training ground complex looking exhausted, you'll know that Ade Mafe has been at work!**

Mafe was appointed the Head of Sports Science at the club after Robert Di Matteo joined as Head Coach in the summer, the two having worked together when Di Matteo was a player at Chelsea and then a Manager at MK Dons.

Ade has had a lifetime in sport – but not in football, although he has been in this particular game for the last 13 years, working with Chelsea, Millwall and then MK Dons.

Before that, Mafe made a huge reputation for himself as an athlete, representing Great Britain in the Olympics. He became the youngest-ever Olympics 200 metres finalist, aged 18, at the 1984 Los Angeles games and also won medals at the Commonwealth Games,

Mafe still holds the world indoor record, along with team-mates Linford Christie, Darren Braithwaite and John Regis, for the 4 x 200 metres relay - set in March 1991.

So if any players think that running away from training sessions is going to work – think again! Ade's gonna catch you!

# CROSSWORD

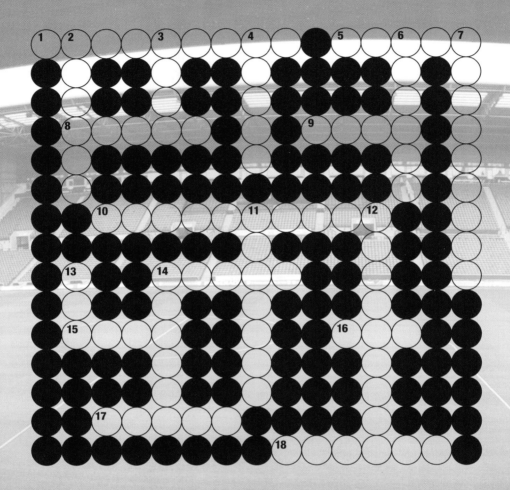

## ACROSS

**1** Albion's greatest goalscorer
**5** Famous striker, Cyrille ____
**8** Bob Taylor's nickname
**9** Goalkeeper Kiely
**10** Our top scorer in the 08/09 season
**14** Striker Luke, signed from the Villa
**15** Mr Clement's first name
**16** ____ Hartford, Scottish star from the 1970s
**17** Our first opponents at the new Wembley
**18** Goalkeeper Scott

## DOWN

**2** Defender Jonas
**3** Navy ____ & white stripes
**4** Colour of our home shorts
**6** Full-back Zuiverloon
**7** One end of the ground
**11** Leon's surname
**12** Our nickname
**13** Former midfielder and local radio man ____ Hamilton
**14** Albion striker, Ishmael who?

ANSWERS ON P61

# WHOLE TRUTH!

## JONAS OLSSON

**Who first kicked a ball around with you?**
My Dad, Lennart. He used to play football too but went on to coach Landskroma Bols, where I also played. When I was about four or five I was with him at the Stadium and we had a kick around there.

**Did you play in your school football team and if so from what age and what position?**
We don't have any school football teams, you only train at school you don't play matches. But I played for my local town's team when I was about five. Then I went to youth academy when I was about 11. I played striker, which everybody wanted to play, to try to score goals.

**What is your favourite stadium other than The Hawthorns?**
Growing up, Manchester United was my favourite team so I must say Old Trafford.

**Who is your biggest influence in the game?**
My dad is. He comes over to see me, and he was here over Christmas. He knows a lot about football as he has been playing and coaching his whole life. It is easy to talk with him about football as he understands.

**If you could choose one player in World football to come to Albion, who would it be?**
Zlatan Ibrahimović, he is a good player and it would be nice to have another Swede around.

# PLAYER PROFILES

## SCOTT CARSON
**POSITION:** Goalkeeper
**BIRTHDATE:** 3/9/85
**NATIONALITY:** English
**ALBION APPEARANCES:** 39
**ALBION GOALS:** 0

Scott became the first Albion player to represent England in 24 years last season when he came on as a second half substitute against Germany. A giant presence between the posts, Carson enjoyed a consistent first season with the Throstles after spending the previous couple of years out on loan with Charlton Athletic and Aston Villa. He joined the Baggies from Liverpool in a £3.25million move from Liverpool in the summer of 2008.

## DEAN KIELY

**POSITION:** Goalkeeper
**BIRTHDATE:** 10/10/70
**NATIONALITY:** Irish
**ALBION APPEARANCES:** 79
**ALBION GOALS:** 0

Dean had to spend much of last season on the bench after the arrival of Scott Carson, but he continued to train and work with the same professionalism and dedication that have been the hallmarks of a long career in the game. When Kiely finally did get his chance in the team, he produced a man of the match display against Wigan and kept Carson out of the side for the final games that followed.

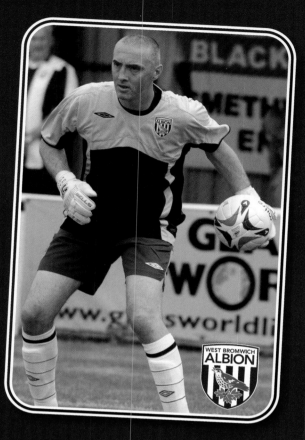

## GIANNI ZUIVERLOON

**POSITION:** Right-back
**BIRTHDATE:** 30/12/86
**NATIONALITY:** Dutch
**ALBION APPEARANCES:** 34+1
**ALBION GOALS:** 1

Gianni made a massive impression at The Hawthorns following his £3.2million move from Heerenveen in the summer of 2008, keeping the likes of Ashley Young, Stewart Downing and Cristiano Ronaldo quiet early in the season. Having had no break last summer given that he played in the Olympics for the Dutch, tiredness kicked in as the season went on but there's no doubting that Zuiverloon will be a huge Albion asset in the years to come.

## ABDOULAYE MEITE
**POSITION: Centre-half**
**BIRTHDATE: 6/10/80**
**NATIONALITY: Ivorian**
**ALBION APPEARANCES: 19**
**ALBION GOALS: 0**

The giant defender from the Ivory Coast joined the Baggies from Bolton Wanderers for £2million in August 2008 and was a substantial presence at the heart of the defence alongside Jonas Olsson for much of the season. A string of niggling injuries did knock his season about however and Meite rarely had the chance to get a really lengthy run of games under his belt. An international colleague of Didier Drogba, he'll be looking to take part in the World Cup next summer.

## SHELTON MARTIS
**POSITION: Defender**
**BIRTHDATE: 29/11/82**
**NATIONALITY: Dutch Antilles**
**ALBION APPEARANCES: 9+1**
**ALBION GOALS: 0**

After almost two seasons in the shadows at The Hawthorns, Shelton Martis had his chance in the limelight towards the end of the 2008/09 season when he partnered Jonas Olsson at the heart of the Throstles' defence. The former Hibernian and PSV Eindhoven man also had a spell on loan at Doncaster Rovers as well as representing his national side, the Dutch Antilles, over the course of last season.

## JONAS OLSSON
**POSITION:** Centre-half
**BIRTHDATE:** 10/3/83
**NATIONALITY:** Swedish
**ALBION APPEARANCES:** 29
**ALBION GOALS:** 3

Jonas enjoyed perhaps as strong a season as any of the Albion players last year and had he not been missing for a couple of months from mid-January, perhaps the Throstles would have collected the extra points they needed to stay in the top division. Dominant in the air, a good passer of the ball and a real leader too, Olsson, signed for just £800,000 in August 2008, looks as if he might be one of Albion's biggest bargain buys in many years.

## LEON BARNETT
**POSITION:** Centre-half
**BIRTHDATE:** 30/11/85
**NATIONALITY:** English
**ALBION APPEARANCES:** 47+3
**ALBION GOALS:** 3

Albion's £2.5million signing from Luton Town had a tough second season at the club, unable to nail down a regular starting place after the Baggies drafted in Jonas Olsson and Abou Meite to play at the back. Injuries didn't help him either, but nevertheless, exposure to Premier League strikers will have been a valuable learning experience for Barnett who will take those lessons on to become an influential figure in the Championship once again.

## NEIL CLEMENT
**POSITION:** Defender
**BIRTHDATE:** 3/10/78
**NATIONALITY:** English
**ALBION APPEARANCES:** 275+25
**ALBION GOALS:** 26

In spite of enduring abysmal luck with injuries in the last three seasons, Clem has still played more games and scored more goals for the Throstles than any other current player. He missed the entire 2008/09 Premier League campaign with a knee injury having only played a handful of games in the two previous seasons, his experience helping guide the Baggies to the Premier League. As a former playing colleague of head coach Di Matteo at Chelsea, he'll be hoping for better things this season!

## MAREK CECH
**POSITION:** Full-back
**BIRTHDATE:** 18/1/83
**NATIONALITY:** Slovakia
**ALBION APPEARANCES:** 6+5
**ALBION GOALS:** 0

Marek endured a frustrating first season in England after his £1.4million move from Portuguese champions Porto. Kept out of the team by the established Albion left-back Paul Robinson, Cech rarely had the chance to show the Albion fans what he can do, but a terrific display against Tottenham at Christmas underlined the fact that if he does get a chance to play, Marek is a very gifted footballer indeed.

## ROBERT KOREN
**POSITION: Midfielder**
**BIRTHDATE: 20/9/80**
**NATIONALITY: Slovenian**
**ALBION APPEARANCES: 100+10**
**ALBION GOALS: 14**

The captain of the Slovenian national side, Robert was consistency itself once again as Albion took on the Premier League in 2008/09, winning great reviews up and down the country and being chosen as the "Player of the Year" by the Supporters' Club. Koren has been one of Albion's most influential performers over the last couple of seasons, scoring plenty of goals from midfield and the Throstles will be looking to him to maintain that form at the heart of another promotion push.

## CHRIS BRUNT
**POSITION: Winger**
**BIRTHDATE: 14/12/84**
**NATIONALITY: Northern Irish**
**ALBION APPEARANCES: 56+23**
**ALBION GOALS: 13**

The top goalscorer and the club's official "Player of the Year" in the recent Premier League season, Chris was one of a number of players who found himself getting more and more comfortable with playing at the top level as the season wore on. After he switched to playing on the right hand side of midfield, the goals started flying in as he got the opportunity to use his famous left foot by coming inside from the wing and shooting for goal rather than putting in crosses from the left.

## KIM DO-HEON

**POSITION:** Midfielder
**BIRTHDATE:** 14/7/82
**NATIONALITY:** South Korean
**ALBION APPEARANCES:** 13+13
**ALBION GOALS:** 2

Kim suffered a horrible injury early on last season as Albion won 1-0 up at Middlesbrough, and that had a big impact on his campaign as he struggled to break back into the team when he was fit again. A composed midfielder with a good range of passing, Kim is still waiting to really establish himself in the Albion side, but he has the talent and the international experience to make a big contribution if he gets the opportunity.

## GRAHAM DORRANS

**POSITION:** Midfielder
**BIRTHDATE:** 5/5/87
**NATIONALITY:** Scottish
**ALBION APPEARANCES:** 6+5
**ALBION GOALS:** 0

Dorrans made a big impression in his first season at The Hawthorns. Although he was expected to be little more than a bit part player, a number of strong displays as a substitute paved the way for him to come into the team in the later games of the season and become a big favourite with Albion supporters with his calm, controlled performances in central midfield. Graham's aim will be to become a first team regular this season and to push himself into the international reckoning too.

## FILIPE TEIXEIRA
**POSITION:** Midfielder
**BIRTHDATE:** 2/10/80
**NATIONALITY:** Portuguese
**ALBION APPEARANCES:** 34+16
**ALBION GOALS:** 5

The Premier League season was a very frustrating one for Teixeira who couldn't quite get back to full fitness in time to play a real part, still coming back from the cruciate knee injury he suffered as the Throstles won promotion the year before. Teixeira's talent is never in question, the supporters love him, and a fully fit Filipe will be a big asset to Albion as they look to win promotion this season.

## JAMES MORRISON
**POSITION:** MIDFIELDER
**BIRTHDATE:** 25/5/86
**NATIONALITY:** SCOTTISH
**ALBION APPEARANCES:** 61+12
**ALBION GOALS:** 9

James started the Premier League season with a burst of goals, mainly against a team wearing claret and blue – West Ham and Aston Villa. He won a place in the Scottish national side too, appearing in their World Cup qualifiers as he completed another consistent season in the Albion midfield, appearing mainly on the right hand side, though he later swapped flanks with Chris Brunt to good effect.

## BORJA VALERO
**POSITION: MIDFIELDER**
**BIRTHDATE: 12/1/85**
**NATIONALITY: SPANISH**
**ALBION APPEARANCES: 29+5**
**ALBION GOALS: 0**

Albion's record signing at £4.7million joined us from Real Mallorca in August 2008 having played for the Spanish outfit at The Hawthorns earlier that month in a pre-season friendly. Valero showed great touch and vision in the centre of the Albion midfield although it took him time to get used to the pace and physical power of the Premier League. He was beginning to show us his very best football towards the end of the season and will be hoping to maintain that progress this season.

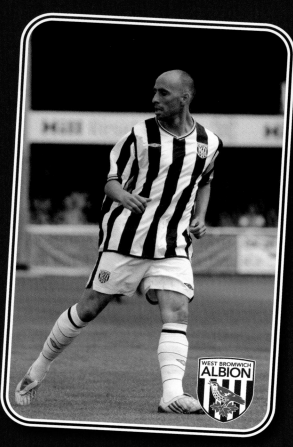

## LUKE MOORE
**POSITION: STRIKER**
**BIRTHDATE: 13/2/86**
**NATIONALITY: ENGLISH**
**ALBION APPEARANCES: 10+23**
**ALBION GOALS: 1**

Finding himself starting from the substitutes' bench more often than not since he joined Albion from Aston Villa, Moore has only been able to give the Baggies' supporters the occasional glimpse of his undoubted pace and power. The composed finish that brought him his first Albion goal against Manchester City, along with impressive late shows against both Everton and Liverpool, showed just what he can do, so the Throstles will be looking to him for plenty of Championship goals this season.

# ISHMAEL MILLER

**POSITION:** Striker
**BIRTHDATE:** 5/3/87
**NATIONALITY:** English
**ALBION APPEARANCES:** 39+16
**ALBION GOALS:** 19

Ishmael was really beginning to find his feet as a Premier League striker when he suffered knee damage after a collision with Portsmouth's David James in December 2008. That ruled him out for the rest of the season but the big striker recovered in time to be ready for pre-season training, only to be sidelined all over again by a second operation that ruled him out for the start of the Championship campaign.

# CRAIG BEATTIE

**POSITION:** Striker
**BIRTHDATE:** 16/1/84
**NATIONALITY:** Scottish
**ALBION APPEARANCES:** 11+25
**ALBION GOALS:** 5

Craig spent a lot of last season on loan, out at Crystal Palace and Sheffield United, where he proved himself a very handy Championship goalscorer indeed, still finding time to fit in a return to The Hawthorns where he notched his first Premier League goal in the 2-0 victory over Tottenham last Christmas. The former Celtic striker will be looking to make his mark on the Baggies this season in his third season south of the border.

# GOAL OF THE SEASON

**It was a tough season back in the Premier League for the Baggies but there were plenty of bright spots – such as the fact that Ishmael Miller proved he could score goals at the top level.**

Who knows what might have happened to Albion if Ish hadn't got injured, but before he was ruled out for the second half of the season, the big man still had time to register the Throstles' goal of the season – and what a goal it was!

It came against Blackburn Rovers, just past the hour mark, with the scores locked at 1-1. Collecting a pass from Jonathan Greening, Miller turned and struck a fierce shot from the edge of the box all in the same movement.

Rovers 'keeper Paul Robinson never saw it as it flashed past him – a goal of real quality from Ishmael. Let's hope for plenty more to come!

# QUIZ **ANSWERS**

## GETTING FROM A TO Z p26

1  Osvaldo Ardiles
2  Baggies
3  Scott Carson
4  Dublin
5  Everton
6  Five
7  Jonathan Greening
8  The Hawthorns
9  Iceland
10  Jeff
11  Kidderminster Harriers
12  Lillestrom
13  Miller
14  Newcastle United
15  Jonas Olsson
16  Preston North End
17  Queens Park Rangers
18  Bryan Robson
19  Smethwick End
20  The Throstles
21  Ifeanyi Udeze
22  Borja Valero
23  John Wile
24  X-ray
25  Youth team
26  Gianni Zuiverloon

## WHAT HAPPENED TO YOU? p29

1  Scott Carson
2  Luke Moore
3  Graham Dorrans
4  James Morrison
5  Shelton Martis
6  Gianni Zuiverloon

## WORDSEARCH p40

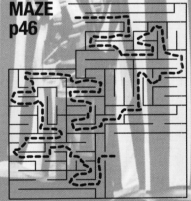

## MAZE p46

## CROSSWORD p48

Across:
1  Tony Brown
5  Regis
8  Super
9  Dean
10  Chris Brunt
14  Moore
15  Neil
16  Asa
17  Derby
18  Carson

Down:
2  Olsson
3  Blue
4  White
6  Gianni
7  Smethwick
11  Barnett
12  Throstles
13  Ian
14  Miller